# 60 Second Tarot

## THE QUICK ROAD TO MASTERY

ANMARIE UBER

TUGGLE
publishing
QUALITY CONTENT THAT CHANGES LIVES

# Contents

**Anmarie Uber/Tuggle Publishing**

**www.anmarieuber.com**

**60 Second Tarot/ Anmarie Uber**. -- 1st ed.

❀ Created with Vellum

*Dedicated to all my students and clients.*

*The road less traveled remains hidden, until the cards are dealt.*

———ANMARIE UBER

# Introduction

Welcome to the world of tarot! My hope for this book, is that you will find reading cards an easy skill to learn. I have taken the mystery out of tarot, breaking the deck down into simple pieces, that can be put together for interpretation. If you have thought that a seventy-eight card deck was too overwhelming to learn, I am here to prove to you, that it can be done! And quickly. The system I have created, is easy to follow and master. You will be reading the cards in no time. *All* seventy-eight of them.

This book is the realization of my dream. To help others read with speed and accuracy. And with or without intuitive ability. No more referring to a booklet, to see what a card means. This system of tarot reading, is easy to memorize, and I have designed it to be able to answer any question.

## MY STORY

I was first introduced to tarot in 1988, while working in a new age store in New York. I was immediately drawn to these mysterious cards, and their beautiful imagery. My first deck was Italian, although I have not been able to find a copy of it in print, any longer. But the cards had me hooked, as soon as I picked them up. I began laying out spreads, but found I had to constantly refer to a book, for interpretation of the cards. Finding this inconvenient, I started to rely on intuition, instead. But I still wanted to learn the traditional meanings of the cards. So, for many years, I followed a book for interpretation. Not being good at memorizing, I failed to learn them. And I was always unsure which meaning was appropriate.

Over the years, I finally found a way to read, that was detailed, quick and accurate. I began teaching the method in small groups, finding I enjoyed that, almost as much as reading the cards. The feedback from students was always very positive, encouraging me to write a book. But I kept putting it off.

In 2005, I had an idea for designing a deck of my own, but never found an artist to commit to the project. When I finally decided to put my classes into book form, I was met with a major challenge. U.S. Games & Systems would not let me use their imagery, without a paying a fee. And they had to approve the book, first. If I got approved, I could only use the images for three years. If they decided not re-sign me after three years, I would have to pull my book. I was at their mercy. And rumor has it that the fee goes up, significantly, with each renewal. I'm not sure what their requirements are currently, but this was definitely a roadblock for the book. I had hoped U.S. Games would realize my book, and others like it, would continue to bring relevancy to the Rider Waite Tarot, as well as help sell their decks for them.

It wasn't until January of 2020, that a friend suggested I forget the images, and make an instructional book with no pictures. He said many authors were doing the same. I would guess for similar reasons. I could always insert my own images later, if I ever found an artist to finish my deck project. So, that is how this book, you now hold, came into existence. Since that time, Rider Waite has come into public domain.

This is the same system I use in readings and workshops. I think you will find my method very simple and accurate. Ultimately, I hope you discover a love of tarot, to match my own. The cards are special to me, bringing comfort, during rough times. And have proven to be an excellent tool, to help decipher what my unconscious mind was attracting into my life, as well as how to break recurring cycles.

Your own journey through the cards, will be uniquely yours. Providing insights only you can understand. Enjoy that journey, as you explore this magical world of imagery, symbolism and numbers, getting to know you, in deeper ways than you imagined.

Much Love,
    Anmarie

Author's note: This book is based on the Rider Waite deck, which I use to teach with, due to its simplicity, and the fact that most modern decks have spun off this deck. I do not sell, or own this deck, but here is a link to buy it. Anmarieuber.net/buy-rider-waite

I am currently working on adding instructional videos for my website. "60 Second Tarot" will become a companion to those. Check back with me for updates when these workshops become available, at anmarieuber.com.

CHAPTER 1

*What is Tarot*

Nobody knows the true origin of the word "tarot", but it sparks many reactions. For some fear, and others, hope. Even though we don't know the meaning of the word, "tarot" refers to a traditional deck of cards, following a set system. Usually used for prediction and fortune-telling. A "tarot deck" consists of suits and trumps – or "triumphs" (see Brief History of Tarot – Chapter 2). The cards are named and numbered, in modern versions.

## A BREAKDOWN OF THE DECK

A typical tarot deck, following the accepted format, consists of seventy-eight cards. Fifty-six Minor Arcana or Pips, and twenty-two Major Arcana, or Trumps. The Minor Arcana follow a regular deck of fifty-two cards, with four suits (hearts, spades, diamonds, clubs). These are usually Cups for Hearts, Swords for Spades, Pentacles or Coins for Diamonds and Wands or Staffs for Clubs. Earlier decks used other descriptors for suits, such as bells, acorns etc. There are four extra cards added to the Minor Arcana. They are the four "Pages", one in each suit, embodying the essence of that suit. The people cards, or "Court" cards in the

Minor Arcana, relate to the Jack, Queen and King. They are the Page, Knight, Queen and King. These can relate to people or situations. The Minor Arcana deal with daily life. The Major Arcana consists of the numbered Trump cards 0 – 21, or 1-22. These cards are archetypes, that can have ordinary or symbolic meanings. They are the heavy-hitters, showing a progression of development.

Tarot can be used for many purposes:
Meditation
Dream Work
A Spiritual Growth Tool
Divination
Games
Magic
The most popular of these, is using the cards for *prediction*.

## DIFFERENCES BETWEEN ORACLE AND TAROT DECKS

Oracle decks do not follow any set format. The imagery, number of cards and meanings are up to the artist of the deck. If, for example, you buy a deck of tarot cards, you know to expect seventy-eight cards, in a numbered order with set image associations. With an oracle deck, anything goes. Therefore, oracle decks may be harder to read, without relying on the accompanying book or booklet, for interpretation.

## HANDLING AND CARING FOR YOUR DECK

There are many opinions on how to use your cards when doing a reading, from how to shuffle and pick the cards, to laying them out. My advice is to find your own method, and what feels right for you. Personally, I fan the deck out, and choose each card individually. While other people would rather cut the deck and deal straight from the top. It is completely personal preference. There is no right way to shuffle and deal.

## To Touch or Not to Touch

Another thing to consider, is if you want other people touching your cards. I used to be more casual with my decks, but have learned that people handling the deck can leave their energy in it, or tie cords to it. So, decide before you start reading, if you want to be the only one touching your deck.

For storage, I put my cards away in a box, after using them. I never leave them lying out in the open.

## Are You High?

I do think that anyone reading tarot needs to raise the energy level of their thoughts to a neutral centered space. Get in touch with the joy of your soul energy and detach from the material world. This clears your energy field. I also advise clearing the deck, regularly. This can easily be done by:

- Placing the cards in a sunny window
- Keeping crystals near them, such as carnelian, real citrine and selenite
- Blowing your breath on the cards
- Holding them near your heart and putting intention into them
- Keeping salt nearby
- Imagining cleansing light moving through the deck and clearing away all interference
- Passing the deck through the smoke of burning sage

- Using black tourmaline, blue kyanite, sugilite and turquoise with copper to remove or keep away attachments, or even clear clients bringing in various energies that may want to interfere with a reading. This can be their own emotions or thoughts, or other people's energy they may have picked up, and carried in.
- Removing any cords to the deck. Remember that tarot is a universal system, that many people are using. A lot of energy and thoughts are going into this system, so a kind of archetypal thought field has been created, that is connected to tarot. Or a thought pool. Some of it nice, some not so nice. Keep your vibration high, and out of that communal energy field.

# CHAPTER 2

# Brief History of Tarot – the Real & the Assumed

There are a lot of sources, that give the history of Tarot, but as we are all aware, history is constantly changed, to suit someone's agenda. It is happening in my lifetime (I am seeing history books being changed so as not to offend people, right now as of this writing...I mean how can you change history?)

People lived long before we were ever here. And there is no one around anymore, who can verify, or give their first-hand experience of the past. *Which means, we don't know our history.* With that being said, we will only talk in this chapter, about what can be proven. What can be traced back to facts. And what is accurate, given the time period, and what belief system would have been in place. Incidentally, that "place", for tarot anyway, is northern Italy in the early 1400's. During the Renaissance.

Robert M. Place brings up a very good point, in his book "The Tarot, History, Symbolism, and Divination", that you can't have tarot "cards", without paper. So, if we trace back the origin of the tarot card, we also have to look at the discovery of paper.

. . .

It was discovered, in the second century, in China, made from the mulberry tree. Paper did not reach Asia or Egypt, until approximately 800A.D. It started being manufactured in 900A.D. Since the original tarot cards are traced to Italy, one has to look at when paper made its way to Europe - the 12th century. To Spain in 1121, to be exact. Prior to using paper for cards, divining was done with sticks, wood, bone, leather, shells, stones, coins and animal skins.

Early card games used a deck of cards with four suits. There is historical evidence that these cards were used for gambling and divination, as well as games. In roughly 1410 – 1430, The "carte-da-trionfi" was created. This was a deck of cards, with a fifth "suit" added, called "trionfi" or triumphs/trumps. So, carte-da-trionfi literally meant a deck of cards with trumps added to it. In 1530, the name was changed to Tarocchi.

The early tarot decks were incomplete. Only fragmented decks were recovered by historians and preserved in museums. The trumps varied, in number and imagery. Some held mysterious cards, that researchers could not identify, and some with cards containing the Holy Grail, and Arthurian themes.

The Visconti – Sforza family were rulers of Milan, at that time. They had commissioned several decks to be made. These were hand painted. One of these decks is called the Pierpont-Morgan-Bergamo deck. It is the most complete of these ancient salvaged decks, and contained six royal cards, or "court" cards, as we know them today. Two Knaves – a male and a female, two Knights – male and female, a Queen and a King.

. . .

The Cary-Yale Visconti Deck is the second most complete relic deck, containing trump cards of the Christian virtues of faith, hope and charity.

The Sola Busca deck is the first deck with numbered cards, pictured scenes on the minor arcana and famous warriors on the trumps.

The Minchiate deck, from the 1500's had forty trumps and a Fool card, but was also incomplete, so its number of trumps is unknown.

In 1507, Marseille, France became the center hub for tarot production. A standardized deck was created, using roman numerals, a set order to the cards and twenty-two trumps. "Tarot of Marseille", refers to this style of deck and format.

* * *

TAROT GETS A BAD NAME

The following influencers, were occultists, and became interested in the Tarot of Marseille style:

In 1781, a gentleman named Antoine Court de Gebelin created his own version of where he thought tarot originated. Nearly all, of his theories have been disproven. But his opinions have shaped modern tarot decks, today. Gebelin was a freemason of the highest degree.

. . .

He commissioned a deck to use for divination and wanted it aligned with hermeticism. His theory was that tarot originated in ancient Egypt. He went on, to further state that the word "tarot", was derived from the Egyptian words "Tar" and "Rho". Later, the ability to interpret hieroglyphics was discovered, and his theories were named false.

He was assigning a Hebrew alphabet to Egyptians, who used hieroglyphics. He also ascribed the gypsies as being responsible for spreading tarot to Europe – being "gypsies" or descendants of "Egypt". History shows, however, that they arrived in Europe, too late to have introduced tarot cards. And their origins were traced to India, not Egypt. Gebelin changed the tarot imagery to make it more Egyptian and switched the Pope and Papesse cards to the High Priest and Priestess cards, wishing to remove Christian symbolism from the cards.

Author's Note: I would be inclined to believe the Egyptians could have been involved with tarot, receiving information from the Chaldeans, who came to Babylonia. It is my theory that the trump cards in tarot followed the fifty-two numbers in Chaldean Numerology. These were in accordance to the fifty-two weeks in a year, which the Chaldeans created. And some Chaldean knowledge has been preserved in India.

Unfortunately, Gebelin produced no source, from which he was obtaining his information. Gebelin's friend, Comte de Mellet believed the word "tarot" originated from the Egyptian "Ta Rosh" – Thoth – the Egyptian deity. This was also inaccurate, although we have a Thoth tarot deck today, and many Egyptian images are still found in card decks. What these two gentleman did get right, is that the trumps were possibly divided into different stages of man, and the four suits represented the four classes of society.

The next gentleman to come on the scene, was Eliphas Levi, in 1854. He practiced high magic. Levi proposed that the twenty-two trump in the Marseille style related to the twenty-two letters in the Hebrew alphabet. This is unsupported, as it is unlikely that Jewish Kabbalists would support cards with Christian, Egyptian and Hindu imagery. And it was forbidden to create images, as this was considered idolatry. He purported that tarot was connected to hermetic philosophies of Alexandria, Egypt. He coined the term "Arcana" because of this unproven connection, so we now have "Major Arcana" replacing Triumphs or Trumps. And he remains an influencer, however incorrect, still today.

Author's Note: I found it interesting, that when I was researching about Levi, who was discussing the Baphomet Lucifer on the Devil card, I saw "Levi" in the word "devil".

This led to tarot being compared to astrology, alchemy and any number of other things. The Hermetic Order of the Golden Dawn and Crowley also related the tarot to the occult, giving it a bad name. Crowley proposed child sacrifice in his teachings. These were not nice people. Their practices led to tarot being seen as something to fear, in the public eye. Being connected with black satanic magic and related practices.

In the early 1900's Arthur Edward Waite, who had left the Golden Dawn order, with Pamela Colman-Smith, created the

Smith-Waite tarot deck. It is used as a standard model today, inspiring many modern decks. It follows the Marseille style. Waite tried to make the Major Arcana fit with the twenty-two Hebrew letters, by switching the 8th and 11th cards.

Author's Note: Even though there is no basis or connection for this leap of conjecture, as we can see by the previous history, that in all probability tarot had little or nothing to do with the twenty-two Hebrew letters. However, since the Chaldean Numerology system that is preserved by brahmins, does connect the letters of the alphabet to the numbers 1-8. And the compound numbers 10 – 52 to the karmic state of souls, these numbers should line up with the Major Arcana, having 52 trumps. We are left with only twenty-two. And Waite made a mistake, in my opinion changing the 8th and 11th cards.

The 11th card, was originally "Strength", which shows an image of a woman closing the mouth of a lion. In Chaldean Numerology, the number eleven is symbolized by closing the mouth of a lion. That what you say, gets you in trouble. Waite moved it to position eight in the Major Arcana. The 8th card was originally Justice, which was moved to position eleven. But eight in Chaldean Numerology is related to the planet Saturn, karma and the scales of justice. I will let you the reader decide, if Waite's theories hold up as valid. As you can see, I don't agree.

# CHAPTER 3

# Reading With, or Without Intuition

A nyone can read cards. There is no special gift required to give *accurate* and meaningful readings, for yourself and others. You don't have to have overly-developed psychic abilities to master this divination method! In fact, you can read just as accurately without intuition.

In this book, I will teach you to interpret the cards, using various tools, such as symbols, numbers, spreads and colors, as well as show you how to read a card that you "draw a blank on". In my upcoming advanced tarot book, you will also learn how to answer any question thrown your way, through the use of these tools, as well as learning the simple art of "yes" or "no" answers. The method I teach, requires no psychic ability. If you have developed your intuition, that will only add to the depth of any reading.

Tarot is a device that allows you to pick up information and translate it to the 3D world experience. Like a radio is used to pick up a signal and play music. Tarot connects you to your higher self, as well as all aspects of the Universe. Any question can be asked.

Most can be answered, unless it is inappropriate to answer that question, such as someone asking for personal details about another person. There may be some information that comes up in this case, but not all.

Now, I must say here, that I believe everyone has intuitive abilities, that manifest in many ways. It will be different for each person. You will have some or many of these abilities already developed, or they may lie dormant and unexplored. Psychic perceptions can come to you in a variety of ways. Some of the common intuitive responses, are having a gut feeling about a situation, or having a dream that comes true, a day or two later. Sometimes we think we are just having thoughts, but it is actually psychic information coming to us. Here are some common, as well as uncommon, examples of psychic gifts:

- Clairvoyance - seeing visions
- Clairaudience – hearing voices; sounds.
- Clairsentience – Feeling sensations in the body, such as gut feelings.
- Claircognizance – psychic knowing, or information that comes to you in the form of ideas, mental thoughts, etc.
- Clairscent/Clairolfaction/Odora Sanctity – Sensing psychic phenomena of perfumes, incense and smell.
- Clairgustant/Clairsavorant – Psychic information through tastes that aren't there.
- Clairempathy – Picking up the emotions of others.
- Clairscent Diagnosis – Detecting disease by etheric odor.
- Psychometry - Picking up information through touching an object.
- Telemetry – Writing poetry from psychic sources.

- Auric Clairvoyance – See auras.
- Teleportation Telekinesis – ability to move objects or self through levitation.
- Geomancy – Ability to see nature spirits and communicate.
- Telepathy - communicating with others through the mind.
- Radiesthesia – Reading rays that emanate from energy bodies.
- Mediumship – Speaking to the deceased is one form of mediumship.
- Bilocation – Ability to occupy more than one body, at the same time, in different places.
- Physical Transfiguration – Taking on facial features of a guide, or of a previous lifetime identity.
- Reading Patterns – Palmistry, Astrology Charts, Cloud Reading, Tarot Spreads, etc.
- *Many other abilities:* Talking in Tongues, Rainmaker, Shaman, Psychic Healer, Cloud Shifting, Remote Viewing, Animal Communication, Channeling, Automatic Writing etc.

Which ones come naturally to you? Which ones would you like to develop? As with all psychic ability, you have to be careful, when letting in outside sources or entities, such as in speaking in tongues and channeling. Our gifts and abilities can be hijacked and used for the benefit/agenda of something or someone else.

## Intuition Test

If you think you have no psychic ability, take this intuition test, to see if you can accurately interpret the meaning of this image. It portrays a version of the Strength tarot card. Write down what you think it means.

**The Answer:** You are correct! Whatever meaning you got from this image, even without knowing anything about reading tarot, was given by your subconscious/intuition. Trust the answer. The meaning can change from day to day, depending on the question you are asking about. So, these cards are fluid. You will see later, how to read tarot easily, using much more than psychic ability. But ultimately, always go with your intuition, when in doubt.

*Now I want you to think of a situation* for a friend or family member, that they need an answer for, and look at the image again. Do you get a different interpretation this time? Are you drawn to something else in the card?

Traditionally, the Strength card can mean many things, such as kindness to animals, love winning over lust, conquering the lower nature, or love conquering all, having strength, mastering the self, etc. I am about to go to an animal communication session today, so if I looked at this card right now, it might convey the message of communing with animals.

Another activity you can try, to test your intuition, is to think of a question. Draw a card, and study it. Then turn the card over or close your eyes. What do you remember about the card? Its number? A symbol? Something in the picture that caught your attention? Maybe it was the overall color of the card? Whatever drew your focus, is the answer to your question.

The techniques covered in this book will add to your intuitive interpretation of the cards. The following chapters will help familiarize you with the entire deck, and enable you to start reading immediately.

\* \* \*

Reading Accurately for Yourself

This is one of the hardest things to do, as emotions or irrational thoughts can interfere with the interpretation of the cards. The best approach, before reading for yourself or anyone else, is to do a quick meditation. This will raise your vibration, removing you from any anticipation of outcomes. Your emotional state will be balanced, and you will be able to read from a detached state. You only need a couple minutes to meditate, to enter an altered state of clarity.

Try the following meditation, or any guided meditation. You can listen here if you prefer. anmarieuber.net/buy-rider-waite

Close your eyes, and take three deep breaths, in through your nose and out through your nose. Deep yoga breaths.

> *Now envision yourself standing outside on a beau-*
> *tiful sunny day. The temperature is perfect. Not*
> *too hot or cold. You are barefoot on grass, and it*
> *feels soft and comfortable. The Sun is warming*
> *your skin. Birds are chirping, and the air is*
> *fresh. A slight breeze brushes past your skin. As*
> *it blows on by, feel it clearing your aura of any*
> *debris that doesn't belong in your energy field.*
> *Any emotions, fears or worries get carried away*
> *on this breeze. You are just standing there,*
> *enjoying the moment. Soaking in the sunlight.*
> *Now feel any pain, discomfort or tension in the*
> *body, flowing down through your feet, into the*

*Earth. Take three more deep breaths, opening
your eyes, when you are ready.*

And that's it. I guarantee if you do that short meditation, you will feel altered. The room will look different when you open your eyes. You will feel calm, centered and in a perfect space to do a reading. If you feel yourself going to a darker frame of mind, such as feeling fear, it may be a time to meditate again, or end the reading.

\* \* \*

## READING FOR SOMEONE ELSE

Warning: Prepare yourself, because if you choose to read for others, you will be getting real people, with real problems. Such as someone's child struggling with cancer. So, you need to take it seriously, what you tell people. Be responsible for what you say.

An example would be, it is not a good idea to say something like, "Yikes! You might lose your job tomorrow. Oh well, sorry about that." And then thank you very much, good luck. What you want to do is soften the blow of that information. Then look further, to see if there is a way to prevent them from losing their job. Is there something they can do to change the circumstances? Maybe if they went and talked to their boss the next morning, they could salvage the situation? Or, if they do lose their job, what is on the other side of it? How can this change, be a blessing, in the end? You never want to leave someone in a down space. You always want to uplift. *This is a sign of a good reader.* There is almost always a way to turn negative to positive. Or see the lesson, in the situation. You also don't want to say anything that would spur the person to take any action, that could be harmful or detrimental to anyone, including themselves. Or tell them bad news they may not be ready for. Like dropping a bombshell on someone, and not giving them a means to process, handle or solve it. Some things have a timing, and the person is not yet ready to know.

Reading for another person, can be a lot of pressure, not knowing whether you are reading things correctly or not. But try not to worry about being "correct" or getting confirmations. You will not know if you are, because you have not lived that person's life. However, they may choose to give you confirmations that you are on the right track. Just trust what you get and say what you think needs to be said. You will pick the right cards. The cards you choose are already determined. Trust yourself and the cards. They will tell you if you are getting interference, as the answers will be a bit wonky, or inconsistent (see "Interference" at the end of Chapter Six).

Know that tarot will show you the alternate paths within your script. When I read for someone, I want to read all possible paths open to them, not just the one they are currently on. The difference in how I read for others, is I do not read the person, by getting in their energy and seeing their thoughts or the decisions they are making right now. If I did that, it would just show me where they are currently headed, and I wouldn't see other options that are open to them. I would like for you to do this, as well, in your readings. Tarot will help you look at all these options, so the person will have a focus, and understand they almost always have choices. And tarot can get very specific.

So, do the best you can and realize that whatever needs to be said, will be said.

CHAPTER 4

# The Fast Method for Reading Cards

To help with the accuracy and ease of reading tarot, it is important to learn the cards and assign meanings to them, rather than relying solely on intuition. This is helpful if you blank out, you can still read a card. And even more important, if you choose not to use intuition.

Please note, that I use the Rider Waite tarot deck in this book, so it may be a good idea to get this deck if you don't already have it. Be aware, that there are different versions, such as "Universal Waite" and "Albano Waite", but there will be color variations in these, so I recommend starting with "Rider Waite". This is an easy deck to learn from, and once you master it, you can read any deck. It is a prototype, of sorts, for most modern decks. The images of the Rider Waite deck can easily be pulled up online, with a search. If you are in doubt, I have a link on my website to the Rider Waite deck here.

The following method will get you reading cards very quickly. You will know something about every card in the tarot deck, *within sixty seconds*, by learning about colors, numbers and suits. Let's put it to the test.

* * *

## STEP 1 - THE BACKGROUND – ALL THE CARDS IN 60 SECONDS

There are a total of 4 background colors, in the Rider Waite deck:

- Yellow

- Blue

- Black

- Gray

Learn the meanings of these four backgrounds, and you will know something about every card in the deck!

*A Yellow Background* – Means something is happening right now. The present. Already happening.

*A Blue Background* – Means something is in the idea stage. It hasn't happened yet. Something that is coming.

*A Gray Background* – Balance is needed; balance has been achieved; strive for balance in the situation.

. . .

20

*A Black Background* – There is darkness, instead of light. You are looking at things from an ego perspective, rather than Soul. This causes ignorance in the situation, meaning you don't have all the information, don't have access to the truth or don't recognize the truth. Darkness is blocking your spiritual sight. Wrong path, or wrong information. Possibly, things aren't as bad as they seem.

I just timed myself. It took me 36.65 seconds to read about the backgrounds, on my computer screen. I can now interpret a meaning for *every card in the deck*, from learning four background colors!

Note that the backgrounds may have different shades or variations of these colors. The cards were originally hand-painted. The Emperor card - #4 – has a yellow/orange background. You can see the yellow lines bleeding through, so that is what I consider this background to be – yellow. The Ten of Swords has a black background, that is turning blue and yellow. Meaning the blinders are being lifted, and you are moved into the divine present.

\* \* \*

## STEP 2 - THE NUMBERS

Now that you understand the meanings of the backgrounds, we will look at the numbers on the cards.

This deck has roman numerals, which is in the "Tarot of Marseille" style. All numbers on the cards reduce to a digit between zero and nine. If a card is numbered ten, it is a "1" again, because $10 = 1 + 0 = 1$. If the card is numbered eleven, it reduces to a "2"; $1 + 1 = 2$. If a twelve, $1 + 2 = 3$. And so on.

So, there are only nine numbers for you to learn. Zero will be covered separately.

Memorize these number meanings, to gain even more insight into a card's message:

- **1** – Means a new beginning. Something brand new. A new start.

- **2** – Means a balance is needed. Two opposing or like forces come together. A bringing together of opposites. Or balance has been achieved.

- **3** – Relates to communication. Some type of communication has been received or is needed. Three also relates to the Mom/Dad/Baby theme, so issues within this model. Or some type of triangle situation between three people.

- **4** – Represents stability in a situation, or lack thereof; security and a foundation to build on.

- **5** – Represents a situation that is in a state of changing to something else.

- **6** - The material is relationships between people.

- **7** – Spiritual lessons are being learned. Spiritual transitions or pauses in time for you to finish the spiritual work or learn the lesson in the situation.

- **8** – Represented as power symbols, such as money, sex, authority. Also, the use of power over others, not owning your power etc.

- **9** – The end of a cycle. Also, higher mind and higher studies. Travel. Traveling to something new.

* * *

Zero

Only one of the cards has its own number, or lack thereof - The Fool. In tarot history the numbered positions of the cards were questioned and a forced relationship to the Hebrew letters was suggested, beginning with with Levi (see Chapter Two on history of tarot). Waite then assigned The Fool zero, followed by many other modern decks, modeling themselves after the Waite deck. It is important to note that the Fool card was originally number twenty-two, coming after the World Card at twenty-one. This is in alignment with the Chaldean number "22", in which this number is represented by the image of "a man living in a 'fool's paradise'. Breaking "22" down, you would get the single "4". So, decide if The Fool is going to have a "22/4" or "0" energy for you.

Zero has no beginning or end. There are many meanings attributed to it. In this case I think it can be looked at like a time trap, where one doesn't escape, but goes around and around. The Fool Card as zero can represent escape from the world, coming after The World card. Wisdom has been gained over many lifetimes and the soul no longer needs to be trapped in a recurring cycle of reincarnation. The opposite of wisdom is foolishness. So, The Fool and zero can allude to the reincarnation cycle, awakening to truth, and then having the choice to leave or stay.

The zero on the end of a numbers suggests the next level up, such as number 1 to number 10. Ten being something new as well, but a whole new level of what happened in number 1, which was a brand new beginning.

\* \* \*

## STEP 3 - THE SUITS

The suits are found in the fifty-six Minor Arcana cards. In the Rider Waite tarot deck, they are represented as the Wands, Cups, Swords and Pentacles. Learning what content or material they relate to, will help you read the cards. They can also help determine a time frame that something is happening in, which I discuss in Chapter Seven, on timing.

- *Wands reveal creative or spiritual FIRE energy.*

This is creative force, manifesting into the 3D world. Or matters that have to do with Soul/Spirit. Life force energy that creates something, out of pure form. The laborer or worker. Opportunities from ideas.

- *Cups reveal emotional WATER energy.*

Emotions are ruling the reading. Feelings, or lack thereof. What you love, is what stirs you. Intuition influencing a situation. Passion or emotion ruling a situation.

- *Swords reveal mental AIR energies.*

These can manifest as thoughts, analyzing, weighting options, using logic or rational means to a conclusion. Swords can represent worries, problems, pain, challenges, fears. Or the determination to overcome these negative thought forms. The world of the mind is in control or ruling the situation.

- *Pentacles reveal physical EARTH energies.*

The physical world and its values. Pentacles represent actual manifestations in the world. Money, objects or something that can be seen and measured as having value.

An example, if you are pulling a lot of sword cards, there is a lot of mental energy going on...thoughts...which can lead to doubts or challenges.

\* \* \*

The Court Cards & Astrology Connections

Each suit has people cards, that represent actual people and situations. Also called "Court Cards". In a regular deck of playing cards, these are the Jacks, Queens and Kings. In the Rider Waite tarot deck, they are the Pages, Knights, Queens and Kings.

You may notice that the descriptions of suits match the element descriptions in astrology, of Air, Fire, Earth and Water. Each of the twelve zodiac signs, Aries through Pisces, corresponds with one of these elements.

This is as far as I personally go, in relating astrology to tarot, other than the correlations of the planets to the numbers 1 – 9. All else is speculation (see Levi in Chapter 2 on History).

- *Fire Signs*: Aries, Leo, Sagittarius

- *Water Signs*: Cancer, Scorpio, Pisces

- *Air Signs*: Gemini, Libra, Aquarius

- *Earth Signs*: Taurus, Virgo, Capricorn

So, the fire signs, Aries, Sagittarius and Leo can be connected to the Wand fire suit in tarot, and so on.

Each suit of "people", or "Court Cards", can be related to a *specific* astrology sign, within that element.

Decide ahead of time, which court card is going to represent which astrology sign for you, so that every time the Queen of Wands comes up, you know you are talking about an Aries person. You don't have to guess. As you become more familiar with tarot, you may find you don't have to do this. The Queen of Wands can refer to a Capricorn, or anyone, at the time of the reading. But in the beginning, it can help to determine which card will be Aries, Taurus, etc.

Personally, I have taken all the cardinal astrology signs and made them "kings". All the fixed signs "queens". And all the mutable signs "knights".

For example, I have assigned them as follows (you can choose to do this differently):
Aries = King of Wands
Leo = Queen of Wands
Sagittarius = Knight of Wands

The Page represents anyone of a fire nature, a fire type message, or a child who is a fire sign.

Capricorn = King of Pentacles
    Taurus = Queen of Pentacles
    Virgo = Knight of Pentacles
    The Page represents anyone of an earth nature, an earth type message, or a child who is an earth sign.

Libra = King of Swords
    Aquarius = Queen of Swords
    Gemini = Knight of Swords
    The Page represents anyone of an air nature, an air type message, or a child who is an air sign.

Cancer = King of Cups
    Scorpio = Queen of Cups
    Pisces = Knight of Cups
    The Page represents anyone of a water nature, a water type message, or a child who is a water sign.

*If it helps you to remember, you can write the sign on the card itself.*

Choosing a Significator

A significator is a card that represents *you*. It is recommended that you pick a King or Queen represent yourself. They relate to the astrology signs, connected to their element. (Note: I have tried using the High Priestess to represent myself, and it didn't seem to work for me. I also chose the Queen of Pentacles, because I wanted to be better in business. However, I ended up using my true astrology Sun Sign card, The Queen of Cups, as I am a water sign, and it seemed to be more accurate. I had to accept the qualities of my card. Just my personal experience.)

I want to talk about the people cards, for a minute. As I mentioned, I attribute all the cardinal astrology signs to the Kings. All the fixed astrology signs to the Queens, and the mutable signs to the Knights. This does not mean I recommend you choose a Knight for your Significator, if you are a mutable sign. Let me give you an example of what I mean, and why.

Let's say you are a Pisces female. You are in the Cups suit, representing the element water (because Pisces is a water sign). Regardless of your gender preference, or whether you are gay etc., you, as a feminine Pisces identify as the Queen of Cups (although you could pick the King, as your Significator, as well). These two are the people cards of your suit and the element of water. Choose one of these. If you are doing a general reading, for yourself, or another person, and the Knight of Cups comes up, this card would represent a mutable Pisces person in the reading, or it could represent situational circumstances. So, the Knight of Cups represents Pisces, but it shouldn't necessarily represent you, to yourself, as a Significator. If *someone else was reading for you,* then Knight of Cups could represent you in the cards.

\* \* \*

Removing the Significator

A lot of tarot teachers suggest that you remove your Significator from the deck, and place it on the table, when doing a reading for yourself. I find this unnecessary, and always keep the card in the deck, for a couple reasons. One, is that someone else may be represented by that card, who is pertinent to the reading. If you have already removed the card, it cannot be used to represent this person. Another is that if your card comes up, it could be telling you that the situation you are asking about, is up to you. Or that you are a determining factor in the outcome of the reading.

. . .

For example, you asked about whether you are going to be fired from your job. You lay the cards out in the Celtic Cross Spread, and the outcome card is your Significator. This means, that being fired or not, is up to you and your decisions, actions etc.

Once you have identified your Significator, study it. Get to know the card. Its strengths and weaknesses. I often will look at my Significator, before buying a new deck of tarot. If I don't like it, I may not enjoy using it.

\* \* \*

Other Significators

If you are wanting to clarify your question to the cards, you can use other cards as significators. Let's say you want to make a trip to the Rocky Mountains, and are asking if this is a good idea, right now. You could choose the Fool card, representing new trips to a mountainous area, or the Emperor, with its rocky background. You would remove that card from the deck, and place it in front of you, to signify the subject matter of the reading. Again, this is not necessary. I choose to keep all cards in the deck, so it can be utilized, if necessary. I feel that my intention is enough, without pulling a card to represent that intention.

\* \* \*

## WEAKNESSES OF THE ELEMENTS.

Fire/Wands – Burn out, using other's for continued energy supply, impatience.

Air/Swords - Bitterness, cold, unfeeling. A need to develop compassion.

Water/Cups – Drowning in emotional extremes, irrational.

Earth/Pentacles – Stubbornness, materialism, stuck in a rut.

\* \* \*

## PIECING IT TOGETHER, SO FAR

Let's take steps 1, 2 and 3 and combine them, to read a card.
    For example, the Ace of Cups:

*Step 1* – the Background Color.

It is gray. This tell us balance is needed. Or there is balance, since this card has a positive image (this could be changed by surrounding cards).

*Step 2* – The Number

It is a "1". This tells us we are dealing with new material. Something brand new. A beginning.

*Step 3* – The Suit

The suit is Cups. This is emotional material. Love. Feelings.

An interpretation may be: Something new that stirs your emotions or passions, brings balance.

Next, let's choose the 5 of Swords:

*Step 1* – the Background Color.
It is blue. This tell us that something is coming in the future. An event that hasn't occurred yet. Something in the idea stage.

*Step 2* – The Number
It is a "5". This tells us the situation is in a state of change. Movement.

*Step 3* – The Suit
The suit is Swords. This is mental material. Worries, thoughts, challenges.

An interpretation may be: Your worries and challenges are going to be changing in the future. Or your thoughts about a situation are going to change.

These interpretations may sound general, but to the person you are reading for, they are very specific. A person in an Ace of Cups state of being, is very different from someone in a 5 of Swords mind-set.

For a final example, let's take a card, that doesn't have a suit.

The Empress:

*Step 1* – the Background Color.

It is yellow. This tell us that this is something happening as we speak. The timing is in the present. It is positive, based on the image.

*Step 2* – The Number

It is a "3". This tells us the situation has to do with communication, and situations that involve threes, mom dad baby themes.

An interpretation may be: You are about to receive news, that is positive. Or, you are about to receive news of a pregnancy.

· · ·

35

It is important to take into consideration intuitive interpretations, even if they go outside of the color and number meanings.

# CHAPTER 5

# The Importance of Programming Your Cards

With seventy-eight cards in the deck, and each having multiple meanings it can be difficult to remember or even decide what message a card is trying to convey.

This is where programming your deck comes in. It is simple to do. In the next chapter, I have given several meaning or interpretation suggestions for each card. Read through these, and choose one or two, assigning them to each card. It can be helpful to pick something that is memorable, as soon as you see the image on the card. For example, you have chosen the keywords "good luck" for the Queen of Wands card. Since there is a black cat in the card, which means good luck, you remember your keywords "good luck" every time you see the black cat, and instantly have a meaning or interpretation for the card.

What you do next, is simply program your deck. Tell it that every time you pick the Queen of Wands, it will mean "good luck". Or it will mean "an Aries person", etc. Whatever your keyword(s) is.

37

So, any time you draw that card in the future, you will know exactly what the message is.

This method of programming the cards ahead of time, works for all aspects of readings. When doing a spread, decide ahead of time what the positions will mean. For example, you see in the Astro Wheel Spread (see Chapter 8), several meanings for each of the card positions. Choosing just one or two meanings for each placement will help you read clearly, every time. Apply meanings to colors, numbers etc. so that you are never wondering or in doubt about the interpretation.

# CHAPTER 6

# Card Meanings

U sing keywords will help you learn the cards faster. I recommend choosing only one or two phrases for each card. Make these the only meaning for the cards so that when you read, you don't have to question the message (see previous chapter). Connect the keyword for a particular card, to its number meaning, suit if there is one and background color. This will give more information about its message.

*The descriptions in all caps, are traditional keyword meanings for the cards.* Remember, pick one or two meanings for each card, and make them a keyword or tagline. Such as the Five of Cups meaning "the divorce card". This will enable you to learn a quick meaning, and interpret with the background color, number and suit. This makes for a very specific interpretation of a card, without using any intuition.

You will be amazed, at how detailed your reading of a card has become. Stick only to your keywords, unless your intuition tells you otherwise. After you are comfortable with them, you can add other keywords from these meanings to your repertoire, choosing accordingly. Also note that a Court or People card may come up to represent a person's physical description, rather than their astrological element or sign. So, a person of a darker skin color, could come up as a Sword or Pentacle card, a lighter skin person as a Wand or Cup. Or as a temperament, such as dark meaning an intense personality, or light features meaning a more laid-back person. Choose your own meanings.

Practice, practice, practice will help you remember these keywords!

* * *

## GENERAL COURT CARD MEANINGS

A Page in a reading represents a child or a message. The suit is the nature of the child, and as a message, the suit conveys the content of the message. The cards that are dealt around the Page, tell the type of message, whether positive or negative, and add more to the information about the message. For example, the Page of Cups is a message about cup-type material, such as love and emotions. A Five of Swords card next to it, may mean a message that causes emotional upset.

The suit of a Knight in a reading, shows what is motivating the person/situation, toward action. Or no action. If it is the Knight of cups, the motivation is love and emotions, that motivate and lead to action.

· · ·

A Queen or King in a reading represents a person. If it is representing someone other than you, the suit shows how that person can help, or harm you. If the Queen of Pentacles, there could be monetary assistance, for example, or someone who is after your money. They affect your finances.

**Refer here for images of the cards, or to buy your own deck.

* * *

## THE SUIT OF WANDS

Related to Work, Travel, Business, opportunities and quick movement. Related to the Fire Element.

Ace of Wands

### A BIRTH OF AN IDEA

The leaves on the wand mean growth. A new business, idea, venture, new ways to market a business, new spiritual insights. Great sexual energy. A gift of strength. The best beginning you can have.

ACE of WANDS.

Two of Wands

## WANTING MORE.

A man of prestige and honor has reached a level of attainment.
He has the world in the palm of his hand. A proud man, in
charge. Alexander the Great, Donald Trump. Life is in balance,
but you have reached a plateau. Looking out at what you can
achieve. Contemplating what is next. Being trapped by your
success. Successful dealings in partnerships.

Three of Wands

## OPPORTUNITIES COMING.

Your ships are coming in. Attainment. However you imagined it was going to be...it will be better. You have more options. What you have been thinking about may have far-reaching results. Going beyond your comfort zone. Stretch your mind to accept more. Get outside the box. Accepting the past. Exploring the unknown. Short journeys bring good news.

Four of Wands

## PUTTING DOWN ROOTS.

The engagement card. This image shows two women celebrating, and a chuppah, which is a Jewish canopy – symbolizing a home to be built. Stability and foundation for the beginning of a romance or engagement. Future marriage. Contentment. Peace. Harmony in the home. Something good taking hold. Going to a conference, convention, castle or fancy home. Unrestrained wand energy. Joy.

Five of Wands

## UP TO THE CHALLENGE.

Changes happening. The situation is subject to change, but something else needs to come into play, first. Other people have not decided. Things are still up in the air. Playful fighting, or minor arguments. Competing for the sheer joy of action. Some difficulty and loss. A creative and enjoyable task that will be successful after minor struggle.

Six of Wands

## A SENSE OF ACHIEVEMENT.

The crown of victory. A laurel wreath encircles the wand, a man holds. People are celebrating his victory. Getting out among people brings success. Get out in your car and meet new people. You may be too stationary in your work. Better business comes to you, if you get out. Admiration, and rewards. Good news is coming in relationships. There is a trip coming in the next six weeks. Assume victory, others will follow. A turning point.

Seven of Wands

## HOLDING YOUR OWN.

The Battle. Spiritual transition. Courage. People are attacking you but maintaining your position. Having an agile mind and body. Adrenaline rushes. Enjoying a fight. Staying on top. Slow progress. Take one thing at a time.

Eight of Wands

## EXPANDING HORIZONS.

Swiftness. The arrows of love will meet their mark. This card has
to do with open air, a trip by air, air travel, something that takes
off quickly, going to a park. Things that float through the air, such
as air waves – radio. Love of the outdoors, and open-air events.
Jousting, archery. The eight here represents swiftness and money.
A journey coming to an end.

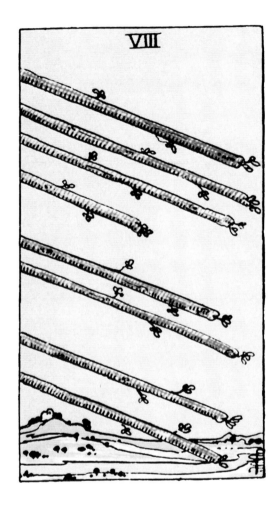

Nine of Wands

## THE FINAL BATTLE.

This person in the image has been beaten up, and wearing a bandage. Could be from a psychic attack, or literal...resulting from the battle of the Seven of Wands. Being on guard. Most of your problems are behind you. Eventual victory, but more fighting to be done. Stand your ground. Don't give up in the face of obstacles. You will reach great heights. Waiting. Such as waiting at the airport. A pause to take time and plan. Being ready. There is something you are trying to move beyond, but more bricks need to be laid. Only seeing enemies everywhere, even though the fight may be over. Feeling restricted, but protected.

Ten of Wands

## ONE TOO MANY.

Doing back-breaking work. A change of residence, moving
furniture, picking up lumber to fix your house. The heart and
back being tested. The heart and back tried by pain. Stressful
conditions. Some kind of moving process. In the image, if he can
make it to the house, then he is home free. New beginnings.
Physical labor, working long hours, willpower and endurance
being tested. Weighted down by problems and commitments.
Doing other people's work for them or taking on other's
responsibilities. Not having much time to spare.

Page of Wands

GOOD NEWS.

*A Message*: The phone call card. A message is coming from far
away. Usually receiving good news, unless other cards around the
Page look negative. Announcing a new project. New work
coming for writers, or those in the communication fields.
*A Child*: A young child with blonde hair and light-colored eyes. A
creative and energetic child. A lively and humorous young person,
who may cause trouble. Having issues with anger or selfishness.

PAGE of WANDS.

Knight of Wands


## MOVEMENT; CHANGE OF ADDRESS.

*Situational*: The Immigration card. Change of residence. Fleeing
a situation. Moving into a situation, and then a hasty retreat.
Adventure. Travel. Liking being on the move. Incomplete actions
or an uninformed plan. Needing a sense of purpose or planning.
*A Young Adult Person aged eighteen to thirty*: An energetic and
social person, bringing love or business. An unreliable or
dishonest person. Having blonde, red or lighter hair, green to blue
or gray eyes, or has a fiery nature.

Queen of Wands

## A STRONG WOMAN, WHO IS NOT EASILY INTIMIDATED.

A social woman, who is energetic, creative and aggressive. Having a warmth, and high sexual energy. She likes to laugh a lot, is a showman and very enterprising. She has an appreciation of life. A dynamic personality, outgoing, good with marketing, sales and helping to promote growth. A fair-minded country woman. A go-getter. The cat is a sign of good luck, and protection from harm. A woman with a fair or clear complexion, and blonde, red or lighter hair. Green or lighter colored eyes.

QUEEN of WANDS.

King of Wands

## A MAN WHO IS A GOOD TALKER AND LISTENER.

Similar to the Queen, this is a go-getter type personality. A fiery
demeanor; high-spirited impatient person. Able to dominate, by
strength of will. Power from belief in his own opinions being
correct. He knows what is true or the best way to do something.
Wanting to aim for the top. Be number one. Talented doing many
different things. A jack of all trades. Could be a Gemini, as well as
a fire sign. A man with blonde hair, or dark. Intense personality.

**KING of WANDS**

## THE SUIT OF CUPS

Representing emotions, love, feelings and matters of the heart.
Related to the Water Element.

Ace of Cups

### A RING OR A GIFT THAT REPRESENTS LOVE AND AFFECTION

The emblem of love. The beginning of a new relationship. A love
relationship. Being inspired. Creative flow. Renewing vows, offer
to get married. A dry spell ending. Happiness. A gift of joy. The
world has value, again.

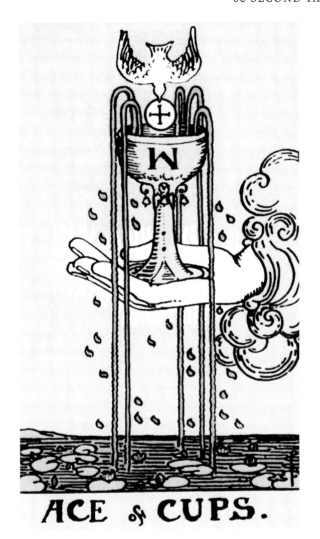

ACE of CUPS.

Two of Cups


BETROTHAL.

The soulmate card. Two opposing forces, coming together in
agreement. The desires of life. Having shared common interests
on many levels. A kindred spirit as a friend or lover. The rising of
kundalini. A future stable home life. Having a spiritual affinity
with someone. Toasting success. The reconciliation of opposites,
settling quarrels or disputes. Someone in the medical or healing
professions. The beginning of a new relationship. Carnal desires.
Having a spiritual, mental, emotional and physical connection
with someone. Attraction. Feel like they know you. The pledging
of friendship, long term union of agreement or the beginning of a
love affair. Celebrating life.

Three of Cups

## A COMING CELEBRATION.

A time of celebration. Announcement of a birth or a marriage.
Going to a wedding. A party. Overindulgence. A communication
of something to celebrate. Work or effort has produced results.
The full expression of the wands suit. Women friends, or relatives
giving support.

Four of Cups

DISSATISFACTION.

Looking for an aspect of enlightenment. Contemplating the future. Not aware of an offer. In deep meditation. A time of enlightenment. Not sure of what you want. Apathy. Dissatisfaction. Bored. Not paying attention to an offer. Emotional security being tested for value. Ace of Cups being offered. Read the meaning for this card, as well.

Five of Cups

## SORROW; LOSS

The Divorce Card. What once was, is no more, and what you will do about it. Emotional reaction to loss. Grieving the past and needing to move forward. Refusing to acknowledge what you have. Stuck in the past. Grieving. Deep regret. There is still a future. Something still remains. What you once cared about is gone, but something new is trying to come in, if you would allow yourself to go forward. Divorce – you or someone you know is going through this. Separation. A loss of someone or something. Being engulfed in the past. Three cups have spilled, due to carelessness, recklessness or not paying attention. Or it was out of your control.

This card is related to many cards, starting with The Three of Cups, because three cups are spilled. So, the vision of that card has been lost. Also related to The Two of Cups, because two cups still stand. Read this card to represent what still stands...the present moving toward the future. Also connected to the pain in The Three of Swords, as three cups have spilled. Read this card, as well for further insight and information. The cloaked figure in mourning black, is related to the Hermit card, of wisdom gained, endings and new beginnings born on the decision to have faith.

Six of Cups

## HAPPINESS FROM THE PAST

Childhood memories. Thoughts from the past. Someone from
the past returning. Innocent love. Taking time to smell the
flowers. A rekindling of something. A kindred spirit. Pleasant
memories from the past. Seeing someone you haven't seen in a
while. Someone you know from another lifetime. An offering of a
new relationship. Childhood affecting the present.

Seven of Cups

## TOO MANY CHOICES.

The world of illusion. Wishful thinking. Choose the unknown, or inner self. Learning to address fantasy/illusion from reality. Thinking of too many things. The answer is not external, it's within you. Psychic gifts, dreams, fantasies. Having visions. Imagination working overtime. Not knowing what is best for you, at this time. Lack of clarity to make decisions. Psychic abilities are developing.

Eight of Cups

## EMOTIONAL WITHDRAWAL

Wanting to walk away from something you have invested a lot of emotional energy into. Desiring to walk away from something or someone you care about, but not necessarily doing it. Looking for desires in a different place. Going to the beach. Phases of the moon, or eclipses. The persona or mask you wear. A fair-haired woman will help you out. Moving to higher ground. A journey into the unknown. Month of August.

Nine of Cups


SATISFACTION.


The Wish Fulfillment card. Emotional and sexual satisfaction.
Contentment. A wish has come true. Winning the lottery or in
other games of chance. A wish of an emotional nature has come
true. Emotional gratification. Simple ordinary pleasures. A good
time. Superficiality.

Ten of Cups

## JOY OF FAMILY

The Happy Family Card. A happy family life is coming.
Agreements and promises made, will be kept. Happiness and
success in all undertakings. A happy marriage. Enjoying pleasant
weather. Tremendous emotional fulfillment is coming.
Celebration, marriage, the completion of something, a promise of
contentment.

Page of Cups

## A PSYCHIC MESSAGE

*A Message*: Dream states. Messages coming in dreams. An emotional offer. Pisces, or the Piscean time period. Sensitivity. Messages of love.

*A Child*: A loving, imaginative emotional child, who may be artistically or musically inclined. Has lighter hair and hazel or brown eyes. Could be prone to tantrums, meltdowns or emotional displays or is very shy. Oversensitive.

PAGE of CUPS.

Knight of Cups

## AN OFFERING OF LOVE

*Situational*: The Date Card. A romantic offering or proposal. A partner coming in. Romantic interludes. Meeting someone at an event near water, a race, steeplechase or event with horses. A need to take action.

*A Young Adult Person aged eighteen to thirty*: Someone with light brown hair, and hazel or brown eyes. Usually a water sign, or having an emotional, romantic nature. A loving person. Possibly escapist, narcissist or noncommittal as his challenges, on the negative side. Lost in the imagination.

KNIGHT of CUPS.

Queen of Cups

## DEEP WATERS; AN EMOTIONAL AND PSYCHIC WOMAN.

Queen of the Mermaids. Meeting a woman who lives near the water, such as a lake or ocean. An easy-going, trustworthy and sympathetic friend. Light brown hair, hazel eyes. Could be married. Someone who lives in a coastal area. Could represent a psychic or ability to see the future. Loving intelligence, with the gift of vision. Could get too immersed in the emotions. May be seeking emotional and/or financial security. Related to the figure in The World card, and The Star Card. Blending the unconscious with the conscious, as she is equally on land and water. The unity of self which brings achievement and the ability to mold the creative force. Also related to The Magician card.

QUEEN of CUPS.

## King of Cups

### A SENSITIVE MAN, STRIVING FOR BALANCE

Meeting someone from a coastal area. A self-employed person
who could possibly work from home. A healer, physician,
counselor, lawyer, businessman, or religious vocation. A married
man. King Neptune. A dreamy person who vacillates with their
emotions. A changeable personality, having whims of emotions.
Nice easy-going person who is sensitive and romantic. A person
who has had to suppress their dreams for responsibilities. A
person pushed to do what is expected. The fish around the neck
symbolizes creativity in an artificial form. Separated from his
imaginative side, with his foundation floating on top of the water.
A passive person who is a drinker. Possible alcohol problem.
"Drinks like a fish". May be unreliable. Can have success,
achievement and mastery in the arts.

## THE SUIT OF SWORDS

Representing truth, troubles, worries, obstacles, health, fears and states of mind. Related to the Air Element.

Ace of Sword

### TAKE CONTROL WITH COURAGE.

Excalibur. Sacred Sword. Sword of truth and intellect. The crown is the symbol for victory. The goal is in sight. You see where you are going. Toward the mountains. Use your sword to cut your way through the obstacles, to get to your goal. Eventual victory, but not without some kind of fighting, trials or tribulation. If there are a lot of sword cards paired with the Ace, mental stress and anxiety is represented. You may have been going through a lot of decision making, or stressful mental anguish. Ace of Swords is clarity. Wanting to understand something, or conquer it. To overcome something, such as being able to quit smoking, or to be more disciplined with diet and exercise. Willpower, determination, valor. No matter how difficult the obstacles, you have the attitude that you will overcome them. Vigilance. You will defeat it, not let it defeat you. The power of the mind, is mightier than the sword. Conquering and victory. If this card is the outcome, you will master the situation, or conquer it. True perception piercing through the material world. Love and hate in their extremes. Old abuses, anger and issues brought to the surface, to face the light of truth.

Two of Swords

## STALEMATE

She has chosen to hold these swords, and could put them down at any time. She chooses to keep the blindfold on, and keep the swords raised. A new moon, or a new beginning. A situation where you know what is going on, but do not want to deal with it right now. Not wanting to look at the future, or too far ahead. A stalemate. Standstill. No forward movement. Just maintaining equilibrium. The sea of emotions is represented behind her. How you are dealing with those emotions – with your swords drawn "en guarde". Detached, distant and aloof -but still "en guarde" – with your armor up. Using all your energy to maintain. Have no energy left for anything else. Overwhelmed. Ignoring emotions. Blocked. Knowing you are in a bad situation but refusing to do anything about it. Needing balance and mental clarity. Your heart is closed off. Vulnerable.

Three of Swords

## MISFORTUNE, LOSS, PAIN, SUFFERING.

Tears will fall. A lack of communication. Unable to contact
someone. Waiting to hear from someone. A love triangle. Three
people involved- you are not the only one feeling pain. Pain that
needs to be felt and accepted, in order to transform it into courage
and love again. The loss or death of something or someone. A
health issue that cannot be ignored, separation and possible
divorce. A thunderstorm, or bad weather.

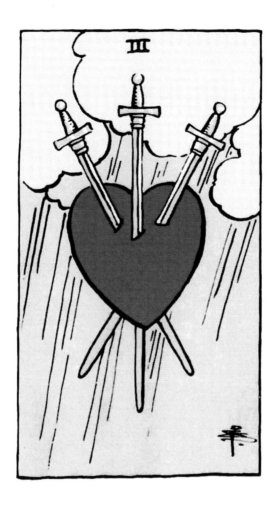

Four of Swords


## RECUPERATION, REST.

The knight has gone into the church, to receive solace and
healing, away from the war zone. Seeking a sense of security and
peace in a sacred place. A time of inner reflection. Needing rest
after a long struggle. Something located in a church or sanctuary.
Going to a funeral. Big cathedrals in Europe. Easter time.
Emotional withdrawal. Cutting oneself off from the outside
world. Needing help from the outside world. Recovering in a
hospital or finding work in a hospital or related healing field.
Connected to The Three of Swords and the Ace, as three swords
hang overhead, and one below. Meaning focusing on the pain of
the Three of Swords, needing to be healed, to take up the truth,
vision and valor of the Ace.

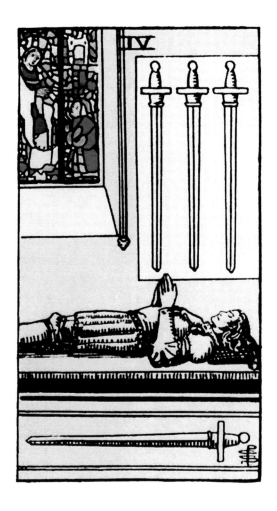

Five of Swords

## QUARRELS, DISHONESTY.

Two people walking off, because he has taken all the swords. The green color is envy. Unfair fighting. Enemies. Someone is lying to you – to your face or behind your back. Sneaking around on you. Something is not working out, at this point in time. A business deal gone bad. Someone has done something, and you find out later. Five is change, which means you will find out, that something is not going to work out. The cards around it, reveal the severity of this card. All negative cards can also be taken in a positive light, depending on the circumstance. Extreme defeat. Humiliation and weakness. Inner feeling of inadequacy. Or these feelings changing for the better. Related to The Five of Cups.

Six of Swords

## POSITIVE MOVEMENT FORWARD.

Ferry boat crossing the water. Choppy water on one side represents moving out of troubled waters, into a calmer and more peaceful situation, or thought pattern. The swords in the boat can represent taking old pain or baggage with you, just because you are used to carrying it. A literal journey across water, such as overseas travel. A change in consciousness. Crossing over to the other side – journey of the dead. Twilight. Depression and other negative feelings finally lift. An overcast day. Weather changes for the better. A journey to water, over water or being near water. A silent passage through a difficult time.

Seven of Swords

## THIEVERY, BETRAYAL, TAKING WHAT IS YOURS.

The Rip Off Card. This person is not using his spiritual knowledge. A plan that may fail. A person sneaking around, underhanded. Similar to the Five of Swords. Adultery. The card of shame. Greed, lying, something deceitful. Not solving anything. Acting alone. On the positive side, this can represent going to an event, such as a conference, and gaining knowledge or ideas from it. Or gaining what you needed. Taking action against your troubles. A daring act or coup. Related to The Five of Swords and the Two.

Eight of Swords

### IMPRISONMENT, DEPRESSION, FEAR.

Things are stressful right now but will not remain this way forever. Being indecisive. Feeling paralyzed by fear. Fears about money, that aren't true. Trapping yourself. Imagining the worst. Humiliation and shame. Confusion. Oppression. Believing you are helpless. Imprisonment or accidents caused by your actions/choices. Fight your fears, and the situation will improve or resolve itself. Related to The Three and Five of Swords.

Nine of Swords

## SLEEPLESS NIGHTS, DWELLING ON PROBLEMS.

Nightmares. Unpleasant dreams. Being haunted by something.
Worrying at night. Unable to sleep. Insomnia. Illness. A lot of
fear. This doesn't last forever. Getting revelations or insights, at
night. Deep sorrow. Mental pain. Mental illness. Seeing the bigger
picture, and the world as a whole, will bring joy and peace. A
mother worrying about her child, or a problem. Things are
usually not as bad as they seem.

Ten of Swords

ROCK BOTTOM THAT LEADS TO RECOVERY.

This person has expended a lot of energy. Extreme mental or physical exhaustion. They may have issues with their energy centers or need a chiropractic adjustment or massage. Back trouble. The collapse of you, or a situation. The future is opening up. You have gone as low as you can go, and things can only get better from here. Moving into a better frame of mind, or physical constitution. The end of a situation. Backed up against a wall. Metaphorically being stabbed in the back. Mental anguish is over. Heavy burdens are lifting.

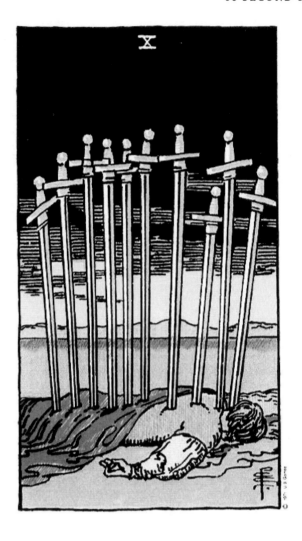

Page of Swords

SPYING; WATCHING YOUR BACK.

*A Message*: Good news comes from the north. Good news that comes in the mail. Messages of written words. Caution or being cautious. Watch your back. Usually represents information coming to you, on some level.

*A Child*: A young child with brown hair, brown or dark eyes, who is very keen in judgement, and has a quick mind. Is sporty, and at times, reckless or mean-spirited.

PAGE of SWORDS.

Knight of Swords

## ACTION IS NECESSARY; DISCERNMENT NEEDED IN DECISION MAKING.

*Situational*: Rushing headlong into a situation – fast and quick. Physically intense. Blinders on, heading straight for your goal. Naivety or fanaticism. Avoid violence, when accomplishing a goal. *A Young Adult Person aged eighteen to thirty*: A young person, with dark hair and dark eyes. This could represent their temperament – the intensity. A very aggressive young person, who wants everything to happen yesterday. Usually an air sign, but with a Scorpio/Aries (Mars) personality. They don't like to take no for an answer. Once they decide what they want, they go for it. No thinking about it, they just do it. An exciting person of action. They come right up in your face. Or a person who comes into your life quickly and leaves just as quickly. A person who could be unreliable, untruthful, or speaks with a razor tongue. A person from California, or somewhere that has trees that look like the ones in the image, or a place where the trees are blowing and it is windy, like Chicago.

KNIGHT of SWORDS.

## Queen of Swords

### A WIDOW OR DIVORCEE; AN OPINIONATED WOMAN.

The Bitter Woman. Often a woman who has suffered from the actions of men. This woman is not looking at you. She has her sword up. The sword has two sides – double-edged. She is either for you, or against you. No gray area. You are on the good or wrong side of the sword. Don't mess with her. A strong determined person. She has faced pain and found wisdom. Possesses courage, honesty and wisdom. Usually with dark hair and eyes. Has lots of ideas. She could be a writer, lawyer, consultant or judge. Her personality embodies both sides of the sword – good and bad. She may hide the bad, or choose which side to show you, depending on her opinion of you. Her challenge is to find the balance, between these two. She could also be a sharp-tongued and cruel adversary. A possibility of mental illness.

QUEEN of SWORDS.

King of Swords

## A RUTHLESS OPPONENT, A CLEAR-HEADED MAN.

This is the only king looking right at you. He has an intense stare, that sees everything. You know exactly where you stand, with this person, because he gives you his undivided attention. Either he likes you or he doesn't like you. It is all or nothing with these people. Black or white. Preconceived notions, common sense and possibly a narrow viewpoint. Humorous intelligence could turn to cruel sarcasm. Cold logic and dictatorial personality, in his negative aspect. He has two personalities, like the two sides of the sword. Related to The Emperor card. Read that card to gain an understanding, if this man is your partner or has authority over you. A powerful mind, intense and very direct in his approach, or how he goes about doing something. A ruthless opponent. Could be a fixed astrology sign, or air sign, such as a Scorpio or Aquarius, Taurus or Leo. Usually dark hair, dark eyes. Sometimes a lawyer, or someone who has to defend justice or decide wrong from right.

# THE SUIT OF PENTACLES

Representing money, goods, property, income, values and the material world. Related to the Earth Element.

Ace of Pentacles

## MONETARY WINDFALL.

The Miracle Card. A gift from Spirit. A job opportunity, money/gift, golden opportunity. A free lunch. Something really good. Spring or Winter season. The wealth of nature. Working with raw materials. Connected to the wreath of victory in The World card.

Two of Pentacles

JUGGLING RESOURCES; SEPARATION OF INCOME.

Having two different sources of income. Two opportunities. Cash flow is sporadic, up and down. Uncertain financial times. Finding money near coastal areas. Ability to keep several propositions going at once. Flexibility and skill to keep everything moving. Having a good time, enjoying life. Dancing. Ambidextrous.

Three of Pentacles

# FINANCIAL INCREASE; MAKING IMPROVEMENTS TO PROPERTY.

Increase in cash flow. Getting noticed, which brings in more money. Getting a promotion, an increase in pay, or media coverage which brings an increase in finances. A master mason, monk, architect or church member. Having stone cut, a new fireplace, work done on home. Getting recognition for work. Studying for school, the priesthood/church, being written up in a newspaper, TV, or receiving prominent recognition. Dedication and hard work results in mastery. Some level of achievement or attainment coming. Getting married in a chapel.

Four of Pentacles

# FINANCIAL SECURITY; GREED; COUNTING YOUR PENNIES.

The Miser Card. Afraid to let go of cash flow. Holding on to or watching every penny. Overly concerned with security. Saving up for something. Having so much money, that you are swimming in it. Work may take you to a larger city. A time when selfishness is necessary. Needing to cover your back. Money may be tight, for a while. Needing to seal or close your aura.

Five of Pentacles

## FINANCIAL LOSS DUE TO FEARS; HARDSHIPS COMING TO AN END.

Poverty consciousness. Believing you are poor or lacking, when that is usually not the case. Dark night of the soul. Feeling left out. Believing others have something you don't. Lovers unable to meet or have no place to come together. Being left out in the cold. Or going to a place where there is snow. Even the church won't let these people in. Two people holding on together, in a bad situation. Hardship keeps them together or becomes a habit. Missing opportunities, because of your mindset. Refusing help because of pride. Five is change, so the situation is lifting. Light-hearted flirtations. A period of shortage ending soon.

Six of Pentacles

## MONEY TO CLEAR DEBTS; DONATING TO CHARITY.

Alms to the poor. Giving money back. Good things coming to you. Unexpected good. Money coming to you from long ago, or long overdue. The scales of justice turning in your favor. The nice things you've done for others, comes back to you. Good karma. Balance. In a relationship or job, it can mean uneven giving. One person is the giver, the other the taker. One person dominates, or is superior to the others, because they are able to give. Those in lower positions of power keeping the situation stagnating. Not being paid what you are worth. Not wanting to improve. Avoid throwing your resources to those who would squander it. Don't give away more than you can afford.

Seven of Pentacles

## HARD WORK LEADS TO FRUITION; KEEP GOING.

Not ripe for picking. The tomatoes are still green. Eventual victory, but there are delays and setbacks. It is not time yet. There are spiritual tests, awareness or acknowledgement needed. You are doing okay, but what is your mission in life? Look within to gain self-mastery of you. A transition from the mundane world, into the more spiritual side. Looking back, with satisfaction on something accomplished.

Eight of Pentacles

SATISFACTION COMES FROM YOUR EFFORTS.

Part time work, commissioned pieces, hand-made/packaged
things. Physical labor. Making something with your hands.
Money is slowly coming in. Maybe not as much as you wanted,
but it will increase. Those you are connecting with will bring
prosperity to you, through networking in the future. Training
that brings discipline and skill. A concerted effort. Carpentry,
mechanical or working with tools. Getting teeth fixed. Going to
the dentist. Needing surgery.

Nine of Pentacles

## ABUNDANCE IN LIFESTYLE. IMPROVEMENT IN FINANCES.

A woman of authority, enjoying her garden. An older mature garden taking care of itself. A level of attainment. A pause in life; taking a break. Completion. Being single. Aloneness. Attaining a certain status, where things are taking care of themselves. Things manifest quicker. Being secure with what one has. Alone for now, but this will be changing. Buying goods for the home. Improvement in your way of life.

Ten of Pentacles

## FOUNDING A DYNASTY. ANCESTORS.

The ten is higher than the one. A new cycle or level of attainment.
A large sum of money coming in from a big sale, such as selling a
house, car, or receiving an inheritance. Happiness and security in
the family. Contentment. A family reunion. More money coming
in, becoming prosperous. Things that reach maturity because
they have been cultivated and developed. Old money. Aristocrats.
Family lineage. Going somewhere where there are vineyards,
tapestries or stucco homes. Italy, Spain, Florida, Napa Valley.

Page of Pentacles

## SMALL INCREASES.

*A Message*: A message about money. Being in school or going back to school. Receiving money for schooling. A small increase in finances. Continuing Education or taking classes that spark an interest. An opportunity at ground level holding promise for the future. Good news, regarding children. Children having success with their ventures.

*A Child*: A materialistic, methodical studious child with dark hair and dark eyes. A scholarly young person, who is serious in nature. A stubborn or selfish child.

PAGE of PENTACLES.

Knight of Pentacles

## SLOW PROGRESS THAT LEADS TO REWARDS.

*Situational*: A business opportunity or sum of money coming to you. Searching for real estate, or property changing hands. A slow steady income. Slow progress, leading to eventual rewards. Offering of money. Dating someone younger than you. A signal of spring, a time for tilling the fields and planting crops. The richness of the earth.

*A Young Adult Person aged eighteen to thirty*: A young adult with dark or brown hair, dark eyes who is easy-going, slow-moving and methodical. Usually, an earth sign or is a very grounded person. Could be tight-fisted, materialistic or after what you can give him.

**KNIGHT of PENTACLES.**

## Queen of Pentacles

### A WOMAN IN CONTROL OF FINANCES.

A dark haired, dark-eyed woman who is good-hearted, down-to-earth and practical. Methodical, yet easy-going, she is an extremely good business woman who can be very helpful to others. A woman offering you a business opportunity. She is good with money management. Can be a good patron. A very established person, with big bucks. Honest and reliable. Can place a false value on money, making it the main focus of life. A tendency toward materialism. A woman who marries for money.

QUEEN of PENTACLES

King of Pentacles

## A MAN OF RESPONSIBILITIES AND RESOURCES.

The Good Husband Card. A man with dark hair and dark eyes, who has already established himself. Could be a Taurus, or earth sign. He is usually married, or makes a good partner, because he takes responsibility for those in his care. Dependable and hardworking. He could be a mathematician, banker, architect or deal in investments and real estate. Mucho dinero. Living off royalties. A man brining an opportunity to you. He may be materialistic, and "all about the money", as a partner. Possibly lacking in emotional or spiritual depth. A real estate or land opportunity. A business partner. Vineyards of Europe.

**KING of PENTACLES.**

## THE MAJOR ARCANA

Archetypes of human behavior, growth and development.

0/22 – The Fool

### A BEGINNING, A FRESH START.

A new state of being. A new outlook. A new way of life. The
beginning of creative force into physical form. Innocence. A
journey. The subconscious mind. All knowledge is with this
individual. They have conquered the world and can decide
whether to come back for another lifetime. A whole new
beginning. Taking a risk. Something being introduced, that the
individual was unaware of. Doing something you've never done
before. A new trip. Going to the Swiss Alps, Colorado, Pyrenees
Mountains, or somewhere with snow-capped mountains. A trip
to the mountains or living in the mountains. Loyalty. Living in a
"fool's paradise". The Fool has the King's ear, meaning he has
wisdom of the world, and chooses to denounce its entrapments.

O

THE FOOL.

1 – The Magician

## PUTTING SKILLS TO WORK.

I am that I am. A starting point. Can be a black or white magician. Physical life force and the material world. Manipulating the life force. Having everything you need, to accomplish your desires. Infinite knowledge. Clairvoyance. The card of the inventor. Someone with original ideas. All new beginnings. New things manifesting. An idea takes shape. The ability to manifest. The conscious mind.

THE MAGICIAN.

2 – The High Priestess

## INTUITION; WISDOM.

The female counterpart to the Magician. The virgin female. The unmanifested. The subconscious mind. Things that happen at night. Other worlds, other dimensions. Receiving energy from the Universe. She has the knowledge of the Universe in her scroll. The secrets. Hidden things about a situation, that is undetermined – the Universe hasn't even decided yet. Working at night. Using balance and objectivity. In a man's spread it represents the ideal woman that all mean dream of having. In a woman's spread it represents the mistress – the other woman. A partner may be unfaithful. Woman of the night, woman of mystery. Highly intuitive person.

THE HIGH PRIESTESS.

3 – The Empress

## ABUNDANCE; FERTILITY.

The pregnant mother, no longer the virgin. A prosperous time, things are growing. The Venus symbol represents May or October, or Taurus and Libra. Harvest time in spring or autumn. Happiness in marriage. Cash flow, abundance. Marriage, wealth, prosperity. The stream of unconscious never-ending flow. The fullness of life. Bountiful. Horn of Plenty. Hearing from someone. Pregnancy.

4 – The Emperor

## TAKING CHARGE.

The husband of The Empress. A man in a position of power. An authority figure. Taking charge and mastering a situation. Having the physical world in the palm of your hand. In a woman's spread – a man who is very close to her. Someone who takes care of those he is responsible for. A person who has a nature of being stable and secure, or on the flip side, is controlling, manipulating and abusive.

## 5 – The Heirophant

### SEEKING SPIRITUAL OR INTELLECTUAL ADVICE.

The gatekeeper to the illusions and mysteries, who has knowledge of the esoteric and exoteric. The guard to the temple, and whether you will be let in or not. Being marked by destiny. Giving a blessing. Being at a crossroads. Whether to conform, or not conform. Whether to go with society or be a maverick. A marriage that is ordained by heaven. A fated, destined relationship. Seeking guidance and counsel from leaders in religious, spiritual or other positions in life.

6 – The Lovers

## LOVE, SEX, HARMONY, CHOICES.

Adam and Eve with Archangel Raphael. Mount Parnassus in the background. The woman has the right to say "no". Eve is looking up to see if she should consent to Adam. The Tree of Knowledge of good and evil. The beginning of a relationship, attraction or sexual relationship. Two things equally tempting. Two situations that are equally good, and having difficulty deciding. No wrong decisions. With a lot of surrounding cup cards, the person is asking about a relationship. Being married and tempted. Having more than one choice, too many choices, or your current situation is not the only choice.

7 – The Chariot


TRAVEL, VICTORY, CONFLICT.

Destiny guided by astral influences. Wanting to control a situation. Someone who has conquered a situation. Means of transportation. Sitting still. A person with bisexual tendencies or preferences. Duality. Gaining control of a situation, or your destiny.

8 – Strength

## HEALTH, ENDURANCE, DIPLOMACY.

The Enchantress. A female master between this world and the next. Can close the mouth of the lion, without brute force. Love conquers all. Conquering the lower nature. A card of sex. Fulfilling sex. Using sex as a great creative source. Mastery of a situation. The ability to master anything on the physical dimension. A physical adept. A person with a lot of strength and willpower. Going to Africa or the zoo. Relating to animals.

9 – The Hermit

## RETREAT, REFLECTION.

Receiving unseen help. Spirit Guides coming to help. A time when your faith is tested. Feeling closer to Source/Creator. When things don't work out, have faith. When nothing makes sense, believe. Build it, and they will come. Feeling as if there is no evidence or sign that something could happen. Have faith.

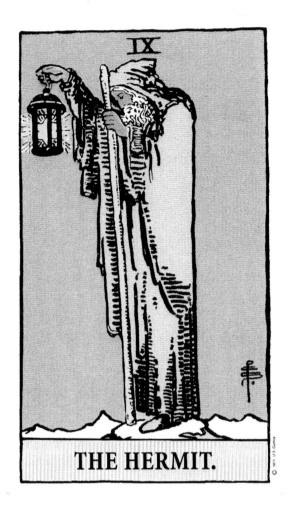

10 – The Wheel of Fortune

## CHANGE.

A change of fate or destiny. Unexpected change of fortune. Usually a positive card. Something is going to change the way you think about a situation. Something coming for your highest good. October brings change. Vegas, bingo or games of chance. You may be too fixed and rigid in your routine. A need to be open to receiving.

WHEEL ❦ FORTUNE.

11 – Justice

## FAIR PLAY, BALANCE.

The scales of justice. Contractual agreements, legal matters, lawyers, having to take someone to court. A well-developed mind is the goal and objective of the individual. Having balance and order in one's life. Taxes. Justice will be awarded to the just.

12 – Hanged Man

## SUSPENSION, SACRIFICE, INITIATION.

The card of the prophet. Suspended time and space. A point of illumination. That which has been foretold will come to pass. Seeing things from a clear perspective.

13 – Death


## TRANSFORMATION; ENDINGS.

The dawn of a new day. Out with the old. Rebirth, rejuvenation. A permanent change that is needed or desired. Sometimes can represent death, if accompanied by other cards that represent pain and loss, such as the Five of Cups and the Three of Swords. No resurrection of something is possible. A replacement of the old.

14 – Temperance


## MODERATION, PEACE, THE RIGHT MIXTURE.

An alchemical process. Changing one substance into something else. Getting the right combination. The conscious and the subconscious mind. More balance is needed or maintaining balance. A time of healing. A hidden influence helping you. New psychic abilities unfolding.

15 – The Devil


BONDAGE, GUILT, BAD COMPANY.

A lack of light. Lack of spiritual focus. Carnal desires. Black
magic, manipulation, control, someone still married and straying,
perverse sexual activities, drinking or drug problem, eating
disorder, obsessions, possession. Addictions. Feeling bound or
trapped in a relationship. Dating someone who is married.
Mentally feeling trapped. Too involved with false power and
control. In a positive light, this card in a past position means
moving beyond something difficult to a better place. Taking
enjoyment in the physical world.

16 – The Tower


## A SHOCK; AN AWAKENING.

The Tower of Babel. 911. The overthrow of existing ways of power. Getting the rug pulled out from under you. A shocking and sudden change. A forced change that you have resisted. Shocking and quick. Loss of job, bankruptcy, an electrical disturbance, such as with a car or computer. Sudden changes without warning. A foundational, flooding or electrical problem with the house. A hidden problem such as a sink hole. Upheaval. Divorce. Eviction. Thunderstorms. A complete change in your spiritual beliefs.

17 – The Star

## HOPE FOR THE FUTURE, DON'T WASTE OPPORTUNITIES.

The great Suns behind the Sun. Other galaxies. Going to a spa, or healing place. An outdoor event. A time of healing, meditation, illumination. A true love that can lead to marriage. A spiritual gift, aport or present. Something nice given to you. Naked. Nothing to hide. Putting money into savings. A happy peaceful card. Becoming a star, or famous. Hope. Rebuilding, after the Tower.

18 – The Moon


SHADOWS, MYSTERIES, LACK OF CLARITY.

Cycles of the moon. Deceit and envy. Something hidden or
deceptive. The moon casts shadows. The card of the psychic. The
astral body, astral planes and dream states. Emotions can cloud
the situation. The good, bad and indifferent. Hard to see clearly.
Not all answers are available yet. The full moon brings news.
Illusions. Female issues. If the Devil and Moon show up together,
reshuffle – this means negative psychic influences are at work.

19 - The Sun

SUCCESS, HAPPINESS, CHILDREN.

Clarity. The light of the Sun lights the way. Conscious mind. A happy marriage. Summer, or sunny weather. Joy, happiness, inner contentment. The birth of a child. The answer is "yes". Success.

20 – Judgement

## FINISHED AND UNFINISHED BUSINESS.

The Age of Aquarius. A higher vibration. You will get some type
of message. Spirit communication. A powerful message,
inspiration or idea. Rate of speed is faster. Something really good
is coming. A state of consciousness. Assess your progress.
Something gone, comes back. Something dead, returns to life.

21 – The World

## BEGINNINGS AND ENDINGS; REINCARNATION, REBIRTH.

Other worlds coming closer to our dimension. Triumph in all undertakings. Blending with universal consciousness. Conquering the world. Your last lifetime. Tremendous amount of freedom, liberation and joy. Completion. Enlightenment. Spiritual knowledge. Gaining recognition. World travel. Taking a major trip. Total mastery and control over the affairs of our lives. Financial, spiritual and emotional health.

THE WORLD.

\* \* \*

## REVERSALS

I recommend using all upright cards, when you are a beginner. As you get more experienced, reversals can be considered. I will cover them, in my next book, on advanced tarot techniques and tools.

Since what you attract, is what you believe, I personally read all cards in their upright position. Occasionally I will read a reversed card, if I am being led to do so, or the card attracts my notice in some way. As each card has a positive and negative polarity, reading in an upright position puts positive thoughts in my mind about the cards. In this way, I will create the highest outcome possible for each card in my future.

\* \* \*

## INTERFERENCE

If there is interference in a reading, such as wonky answers or nothing fitting together, clear the deck (see Chapter One). Or switch decks if you have to. If there is psychic interference, The Moon and Devil cards will come up together. That is your sign that you need to clear, re-deal or change decks.

CHAPTER 7

# Timing: Predicting "When" Something will Happen

T
arot cards can be used to predict when an event is likely to occur. As you saw in the background colors, a yellow background means something is currently happening, and a blue background means future timing. However, you can be more exact, in your predictions. There are many ways to read time frames. I will discuss numbers, suits, images and spreads, here. It is best, when predicting timing, to use just one or two of these, to begin with, so you are more accurate. Decide ahead of time, for example, that you will only use numbers, to determine timing (unless you have a Court Card). And whether a 5 will mean 5 weeks, 5 months or 5 days. Or maybe a Major Arcana, such as Heirophant 5 or Temperance 14/5, will mean a quicker period of time, like 5 days. This will help you narrow down timing, by programming your cards, ahead of time...excuse the pun.

\* \* \*

## NUMBERS & TIMING

Numbers on a card, can be used for timing. If you use the numbers on the cards, to predict when an event will occur, it is pretty straightforward. A number can mean days, weeks, months or years. Since numbers are found in all four suits, and in the Major Arcana, you could divide this into:

Major Arcana: Calendar Month

- Wands: Days

- Cups: Weeks

- Swords: Months

- Pentacles: Years

This is only a suggestion. Examples of this could be:

Wheel of Fortune (10) – Month of October. Temperance (14) – February (one year, plus 2 months). Or you could break these into single numbers, so the Wheel of Fortune could also mean January (1), and Temperance could also mean May (5).

Decide ahead of time how you are going to read these numbers, and stick to it, every time. Then there is no question of whether you understand the timeline. See Chapter Five, about "programming" your cards.

\* \* \*

## SUITS & TIMING

A common system for timing by the seasons:
  Wands – Fire – Summer
  Cups – Water – Spring
  Pentacles – Earth – Fall (harvest)
  Swords – Air – Winter


I do it a little different. I use the cardinal signs associated with the solstices and equinoxes, and set my suits to the seasons this way:
  Wands – Aries – Spring
  Cups – Cancer – Summer
  Swords – Libra – Fall
  Pentacles – Capricorn – Winter


Choose what season, the suits/elements represent for you! Program your cards, so you know ahead of time, the message they are giving you about seasonal timing!

* * *

## SYMBOLS & SEASONAL TIMING

As you look at the images in the cards, certain things may jump at you, to signify a time period. If your intuition draws you to a particular symbol or image on a card, to represent timing, then go with that. For example, the Three of Cups is the suit of summer-time, but the pumpkin in the foreground could suggest autumn. If you are reading the card in July, and are drawn to the pumpkin, *three* months (the number of the card) would be October, or autumn. Or maybe you are drawn to the ladies in the Three of Cups. They could be dancing around the maypole, which would mean the month of May, or May 1.

. . .

Other examples are the Wheel of Fortune, looking like a giant pumpkin, and signifying autumn. The Sun card could be summertime. The Five of Pentacles is snowing in the card, signifying winter. The Ace of Pentacles has lilies growing, which could signify spring. The Knight of Pentacles could be early summer, or the month of June, with the freshly tilled field. The Four of Swords has a stained-glass window, which reminds some people of Easter. The Ace of Cups has water lilies which grow in summer, and the woman in the Nine of Pentacles is enjoying her fully grown garden in summer. The Seven of Pentacles could be seen as spring or summer, as he is growing something, as well. Five of Sword has clouds that can look like wintertime. Page of Wands could be the heat of summer, with a desert behind him. And so on.

* * *

## USING SPREADS FOR TIMING

A spread can also be used to predict timing, as each card position has a meaning assigned to it. For example, in the Celtic Cross spread, the first two cards laid down, represent the present. The fourth card (depending on how you lay them out) represents the past. The sixth card represents the future, two months out. Any spread can be used, to clarify the timing of an event. A New Year's spread can be laid out in a circle. The first card signifying what to expect in the month of January. The second card, February, and so on. (See Chapter Eight for basic spreads.)

# CHAPTER 8

# Basic Spreads for Clarity

U sing spreads can help you further identify a card's meaning. It gives you a location, time or subject matter that relates to the interpretation of the card. The following examples are common spreads, which can add a lot of information to a card reading. If you are a beginner, I would advise using spreads for every reading. This will get you familiar with the cards, and will help you relate the meanings to a specific area of life, or subject matter. Start with simple spreads, such as the one, three and five card, gradually working your way up to spreads with a larger layout.

* * *

## THE ONE CARD SPREAD

*1 Card Spread*

This is a simple layout, choosing one card to represent your situation, person or question. It can be a little difficult, as the position of the card does not give you additional information. However, you can always give it a focus. Such as, laying the card out, and identifying it as the obstacle to your situation, or as the future, the present, etc.

* * *

## THREE CARD SPREAD

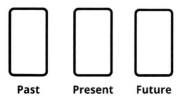

This layout gives a little more information, than the one card spread. You now know that card one is the past, and can read how it relates to your situation or question. Card two is what is happening now. And card three is what will happen in the future, or the conclusion to the matter.

\* \* \*

## THE HORSESHOE SPREAD

*Horseshoe Spread*

This is a great spread, when deciding between two choices.

Card one – The situation

Card two – What happens if you make choice "A".

Card three – What happens if you make choice "B".

Card four – The result or outcome of choice "A".

Card five – The result or outcome of choice "B".

Looking at the cards on the left and right side of the horseshoe, you should get a feel for which is the more beneficial choice. Or, both choices may be equally positive or negative.

* * *

# THE ASTRO WHEEL

*Astro Spread*

Lay out the cards in a wheel, as shown in the image. Each card represents a certain area of an individual's life, similar to the houses in an astrology chart. The descriptions of each house, and the material it relates to, is described below. I would suggest highlighting or underlying one or two of your own keywords to describe each house. This spread is usually used for a general overview of a person's life.

1st – Represents you, your outer personality, aspects of your character and how others see you. Also: Ego, body type, childhood experience, leadership qualities, personality, view of the world, 1st impression you make on others, defense mechanisms, face, body, self.

2nd – Money, what you value. Also: The outer resources available to the individual, material things, safety, security, possessions, attitude toward food with 6th house, self-worth, noble or base values.

. . .

3$^{rd}$ – Short trips, your mind, Siblings. Also: Mental gifts, learning and teaching, school up to college, outside world, cars buses, trains, ability to learn, the way your mind works, positive/negative thinking, communication - writing, reading, talking, teaching, letters, magazines, newspapers, near relatives, neighbors, neighborhood, radio, TVs, i-pads, phones, computers.

4$^{th}$ – Your home, house and what's going on there. Also: Your sanctuary, roots, conditions in old age, attitude toward family, ability to nurture people emotionally, real estate, land, gardening, your father, your mother, country of birth, mines, graves, underground places, quirks or abilities passed on to you from parents, especially from father, genetics.

5$^{th}$ – Love affairs, Children, Thing you do to have fun or love to do such as hobbies. Also: Fatherhood, drama, theater, art, ability to be creative, taking risks, gambling, investing, schools, resorts, games and sports, ability to give and receive love, perception of the love you got as a child, childlike/childish qualities, ability to be romantic.

6$^{th}$ – Everyday work, small pets, health. Also: diets, food, attitude toward cleanliness and order, old relatives, obligations, your employees, ability to be inventive, taste in clothes, servants, uncles and aunts on father's side, community needs, weather as it affects your health.

7$^{th}$ – Partner, marriage, business partner(s). Also: clients, best friends and peers, mentors, live-in relationships, known enemies, dealings with the public, contracts, art, diplomacy, social urges, grandparents.

. . .

8<sup>th</sup> – Other People's money, legal issues, soulmates, taxes. Also: Endings and beginnings, love interaction from the other from the 7<sup>th</sup> house, deep Merging Box, secrets, psychology, therapy, psychiatry, astrology, yoga, detective work, psychic abilities, sex, great change brought about by crisis, death, legacies and wills, hidden talents, ability to be reborn and ability to be alone.

9<sup>th</sup> – Long distance travel, college/university, your spiritual philosophy. Also: Rewards, higher understanding, higher education, mind expansion, gurus, religions, foreign countries, import/export business, publishing, hard cover books, mass circulation magazines, international anything, travel, large enterprises, in-laws, lawyers, judges, lawsuits, the law, faith.

10 – Your reputation, Career. Also: Your role in life, public Image, the parent who was the main authority, credit or lack thereof, people with power over you, bosses, government, attitude toward authority figures, sense of duty, power, public eye, homosexuality, promotions.

11 – Your support network of friends, social circles. Also: Enemies, Idealism, past-life enemies who are now friends, associates, income from main profession, the parent who dominated you, peer groups, advice you get for good or ill, advisors, your hopes, wildest dreams, clubs, other people's children.

12 – Your hidden inner self, that you may or may not be aware of, the inner self that others probably don't see. How we are all one and connected. Also: The characteristics, of your most recent past

life, behind the scenes, God, prison, bondage, confinement, hospitals, large institutions, hidden enemies, everyday saints, psychiatry/psychology – how you mess yourself up, large animals, mother's relatives, escapist tendencies, unconscious, psychic abilities, healing abilities, selflessness, karma and past lives, to serve or suffer, victim, the past.

Card 13, 14 and 15 - Represent major themes going on right now, and usually apply to more than one area of life. One of these cards next to, above or below another card, is related to that card. You can also look at their number and apply it to a house(s) to see its connection to that area. For example: The Sun card in the center is a great card to have as an overlying influence on the spread. Its number is 19, which is 10 and 1, (when added together), so it can apply to cards 10 and 1. etc. Overall the Sun is influencing all the houses because it is in the center.

**The Astro Wheel Spread can also be used to look at the year ahead.

The cards 1 – 12 can also represent the months of the year. Card one is January, card two is February. And so on. Card 13 represents the overall theme for the year.

If you are in the middle of the year, and want to see what the next year will bring, begin card 1 with the current month you are in, and card 2 would be the consecutive month. Continuing around the circle. This can be done, sometimes for birthdays. If the birthday is March 4th, card one will be March, card two April etc.

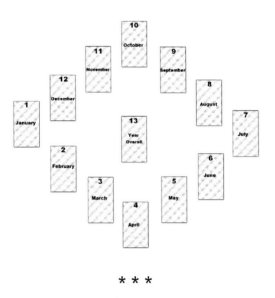

* * *

## THE CELTIC CROSS SPREAD

*Celtic Cross Spread*

This is a traditional spread, that usually reads about 6 months into the future, unless you specify a time frame. For example, you may want to look at a situation and how it progresses over the next year.

## PLACEMENTS OF CELTIC CROSS

**1st** – *The present situation.* What is the current state of conditions around you; your present state of mind.

**2nd** – *Crossing influence* - Influences the situation, things going on, or outside influences determining the situation, or the action you are taking. Sometimes the first 2 cards can symbolize the whole reading, with the other cards adding more details.

. . .

**3<sup>rd</sup>** – *The foundation.* Why you asked the question. Past childhood conditioning. Last few months back up to the present time of reading. What you are still holding on to inside/have not let go of.

**4<sup>th</sup>** – *Recent Past* - What is passing, within at least the last few months back. The same as the foundation, but this is the part that you are letting go of, and what needs to go.

**5<sup>th</sup>** - *Possible Outcome* - What could come about. What could happen but does not have to. Probability of what's coming. If its negative, there can be a connection to the foundation card – what you are holding on to is bringing about a possible negative outcome.

**6<sup>th</sup>** – *Immediate Future* - What will come about in the next 2 months. What you will face if you continue. If this card is very different from the outcome, then this card does not have much, or is a passing influence. If the reading starts off one way, and ends in a very different outcome, then the new influence of something coming in, shown by this card may have changed the outcome.

**7<sup>th</sup>** – *Self or Fears* - What you are apprehensive about? Negative fears. How your attitude toward the future is contributing to the situation, and affecting the outcome. **Often this card will dominate the reading,** especially if the possible outcome (5) and outcome (10) cards are very different (what seemed likely to happen, will not, because of this influence).

. . .

**8th** – *Your environment* – Partner, family, friends, those close-how they view the situation. When asking about a relationship, this card shows what is going on with the partner.

**9th** – *Hopes, wishes, highest hopes* - (Sometimes your greatest hope is your greatest fear– they are the same). Also affects the outcome and is connected to card 7.

**10th** – *Outcome of the question.* – you can look to see what card made it come about, with the hope of changing the situation, or increasing the chances of the outcome, if it is positive.

For further insight:

Compare **card 4** to card **7**. Letting go of your fears ensures you let go of what is passing away.

Compare **card 9** to 7, noting any connections, and how they could affect outcome card 10.

Compare **cards 5**, **6** and **10** and see how card 10 could move into or coincide with card 6, and how card 5 could move into or alter cards 6 and 10.

Think of **cards 1** and **2** as two things happening at the same time with card 2 influencing the other.

Note that **card 3** is who you are psychologically and how you are predetermined to act. These unconscious beliefs/attitudes, as well as your conscious spoken words/thoughts determine and show you what you attract in your life, and therefore have produced the reading.

- Notice any cards that look similar, or have similar themes.
- Notice the people cards that seem to be facing or looking at another card.
- Notice any numbers that come up several times.
- Notice if there are several cards of the same suit
- Notice if there are 4 or more major arcana. This means the situation is already happening according to destiny, and cannot be changed.

Choose for yourself. Consistency is the most important thing. If you decide a certain way you are going to lay out a spread, or certain meanings the position will have, then do it that way every time, or decide how you will do it before you pick the cards.

* * *

## MORE FUN SPREADS TO TRY

There are endless tarot spreads that you can find, or even create on your own. Here are some I like.

## WILL I WIN THE LOTTERY?

First, focus on exactly which game you are going to play. Lotteries are different. The number of picks can be different, as well as the total outcome of your numbers. It may be wise to choose a game is not saturated with people, or a smaller lottery. When you have decided, shuffle the cards, and lay them out as follows

**LOT**

**1 2 3 4 5 6**

The "L" card position, reveals your attitude toward winning the lottery.

The "O" position represents blocks in your awareness to winning or accepting that you could win.

The "T" position, gives you a feeling from its nature, whether this is a good day to buy a ticket.

Positions 1 – 6 are the numbers to play. (Deal more or less cards here, depending on the number required for that lottery.) If you pick the 3 of Swords, the lottery pick is "3".

Add up the totals of cards 1 – 6 (or if there are more or less cards here), and see if the total is within range of the allowed outcome. For example, a lottery may require your total to equal 55. If your lottery numbers to play, are 1, 13, 20, 9 and 6, your total equals 49, so you are in the range, less than 55. Go buy a ticket. If there are higher numbers to choose from in a lottery, you can lay out the six cards, and lay out six more, adding them together. If they are within the lottery limits, go buy a ticket.

· · ·

If the cards you picked, do not give you numbers that fit into the lottery rules, but card position "T" says it is a good day to play the lottery, maybe you should try a scratch off, or some other form of a game of chance.

And finally, if there is a court card in positions 1 – 6, it is possibly referring to another person who should play, or means you can give a number value to that card (an example, would be the page being an 11, because it is the eleventh card of its suit).

The first time I played the lottery, I chose numbers for the Powerball. I picked every number, including the Powerball Number, except one. I looked at the ticket, and it said I had won $10k. Unfortunately, I had Wednesday's numbers, but my ticket was for the Saturday draw. Basically, I got the numbers for the wrong day. I do recommend picking your own numbers, instead of using a computer random pick. This allows your intuition to hone in on the winning numbers. If it is in your script, at that time to win, you will.

I told someone once, that I saw her winning the lottery. She played a couple times. Didn't win much. Maybe a few dollars. Then got a surprise phone call that an old friend had died, and put her down as the beneficiary on their life insurance. She "won" 1.5 million. So, keep your mind open to the ways that windfalls can come to you. It may be in the form of healing, meeting a wonderful partner, or other types of "gifts" as well.

## WHAT IS MY BEST OPTION SPREAD?

Think about your situation, and choose a Major Arcana card, to represent the best outcome for your situation. Put it back in the deck, and shuffle the cards.

Deal the deck into piles. The number of piles, will represent the number of options in what you are asking about. For example, if you are asking which company will be the best to work for, and you have been offered positions at three different places, you would deal out three piles, to represent each company.

Now go through each pile, to see which one your card landed in. That option will probably be best. For further clarification about this choice or option, shuffle this pile, and lay out 5 cards from it.

1 – The first card represents the question, problems or issue

2 – The second card represents background information on the issue.

3 – The third card represents you.

4 – The fourth card represents what the environment will be like, or other people related to the question.

5 – The fifth card represents the outcome, or further advice on this option.

## A RELATIONSHIP READING - YOU AND ANOTHER PERSON

Shuffle and pick 5 cards. Lay them out, from left to right, 1 – 5.

Card 1 – The general situation between you.

Card 2 – How he/she feels about you.

Card 3 – How you really feel about him/her.

Card 4 – Possible obstacles in the relationship, or something standing in the way of the relationship. Or issues that need to be overcome, for more harmony.

Card 5 – Outcome/Advice. Is this person for me? If "no", then lay out an additional card, to answer whether your soul is finished with this relationship, or if there is more you need to go through with this person.

The "feel" you get from a card, will tell you whether it represents a "yes" or "no", in any given circumstance. For example, the Death card may give you a negative feeling, and represent "no". However, the imagery in Death, related to new life, could be feeling like a "yes" to you. Pay attention to your gut feeling about the card, at the moment of the reading.

# CHAPTER 9

# Putting the Pieces Together

N ow it's time to put the puzzle together. Let's take an example of reading a card, by using all our tools and techniques.

You picked the Queen of Wands card:

What we know: She has a blue background, which means the situation is in the idea stage, or hasn't manifested yet. She is a fire sign in astrology, possibly a Leo. She is optimistic, and the cat in the picture brings good luck. Wands is sometimes career related.

Interpretation: There is a fire sign or Leo person, who you will soon meet (because of the blue background), who is bringing good luck to you and your business.

If we laid out cards in the 3 Card Spread, and the Queen of Wands landed in the number one position, it would represent the past. This would be someone in the past, who brought good luck into your business. And because her background is blue, which means future, her influence would continue to be felt.

If we draw the Three of Swords, and it lands in the 3 Card Spread in the "present" position - card two.

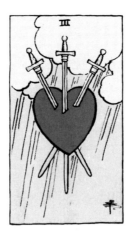

What we know: The background is gray, which means something needs balanced. The number three means communication.

The suit of Swords means problems, worries or state of mind. The keyword for the card is "tears will fall".

Interpretation: Communication is currently cut off with someone, because there is imbalance or inharmony. The imbalance could relate to the emotions or the people involved. Not being able to talk to them, is causing you pain. There is a need to pull yourself back into balance, so you can think correctly and logically (swords) about the situation.

Let's say the Three of Swords was not laid out in the 3 Card Spread (so you don't know the timing). You could say that this situation happens in the Fall, or in three months, because it is a "3" card. Let's say you are reading the card, and it is the month of March. Since March is the third month, it could mean that the situation is currently happening. (See Chapter Seven, for methods to determine timing.) Pay attention to what you are drawn to, in the image. Maybe you are drawn to the heart, in the card, and this makes you think of Valentine's Day. So February would be your timing.

As you can see, with these examples, there is variance in how to interpret them. This is why I stress *the importance of programming your deck,* when you are just beginning to read tarot. Or if you don't trust your intuition. Decide what each card will mean for you, as soon as you buy your deck. *Before you even start reading.* Maybe you plan to only predict timing, with the suits. So, you program your deck, to only show timing with suits. And you consistently follow that method. Now, with the Three of Swords being drawn...let's say in the 1 Card Spread, you know without a doubt, the timing for the situation is Fall. If you choose a Major Arcana card, there is no suit, so the timing could be unknown, or depending on extenuating circumstances.

· · ·

Thank you so much for all your ongoing support, and for purchasing this book! If you enjoyed it, please consider leaving a review.

If you would like to learn tarot please go to my website for updates as classes become available. Anmarieuber.com

# Certification

Thank you so much for your interest in "60 Second Tarot". If you would like to become a Certified Tarot Practitioner, please sign up on my website for notifications when this will become available. I will be adding class modules that you can follow along with to the website in summer of 2021. When you have taken the basic training, as well as the advanced, you will be given clinical work to complete toward certification.

For now, if you would like private tarot instruction, please go to my contact page. Anmarieuber.com

Thank you so much for all your ongoing support, and for purchasing this book! If you enjoyed it, please consider leaving a review.

# *Bibliography*

Bletzer Ph.D., June G., "The Donning International Encyclopedic Psychic Dictionary".

Place, Robert M., "The Tarot, History, Symbolism, and Divination", (pages 5 – 126).

# About the Author

Anmarie Uber's interest in the metaphysical field has continued, throughout most of her life. She had her first remembered contact with the other side, at age three, and an insatiable passion, throughout childhood, for ghosts, UFOs and anything paranormal. Anmarie began exploring astrology and numerology at age 16, and tarot, yoga, massage, nutrition, palmistry, crystal healing, Feng Shui, energy healing, and the philosophy of reincarnation at age 21. Her ongoing quest for spiritual truth has been all-consuming, and has many times taken precedence over personal needs, or worldly goals. What she has found, is that many "new age" belief systems, can be roads to nowhere...another program to be sifted through. Although Anmarie has studied and lived countless spiritual and religious ideologies, the last five years of her life have been the most challenging, as the pressure to keep humanity down is increasing. Anmarie believes in finding the humor in difficult situations, forgiving hardships and lessons with others, and having faith. We are all programmed beings, trying to awaken...and awakening to your true Self, is the most important accomplishment in life.

# Also by Anmarie Uber

If you would like to know more about Chaldean Numerology, and its relationship to tarot, check out Anmarie's book, "5 Numbers of Destiny" here.

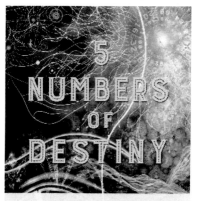

Made in United States
North Haven, CT
19 June 2023

37954107R10135